Unbreakable

A journey of healing, growth, and self-discovery

By Jamie L. O'Neill

Dedication

To all the beautiful souls out there who are seeking healing and transformation.

To my family for always loving and supporting me on my journey of growth and self-discovery.

To those who have challenged me. Thank you for being a catalyst for my growth.

©2024 Jamie L. O'Neill. All rights reserved. *Unbreakable* is protected by copyright law. No part of this eBook may be reproduced, distributed, or transmitted in any form or by any means, including photocopying, recording, or other electronic or mechanical methods, without the prior written permission of the author, except in the case of brief quotations embodied in critical reviews and certain other noncommercial uses permitted by copyright law. For permission requests, please contact Jamie@silvermoonholistic.com

Contents

Introduction
From Rock Bottom to Rising Strong 1

Chapter 1
Understanding Spiritual Healing and Soul Growth Turning Life's Curveballs into Cosmic Growth Opportunities 3

Chapter 2
The Healing Process – Accepting, Acknowledging, and Letting Go Or, How to Release the Baggage Without Booking a One-Way Ticket to Nowhere 7

Chapter 3
Self-Reflection and Inner Awareness Becoming Your Own Best Detective (Without the Trench Coat and Magnifying Glass) 11

Chapter 4
Reframing Setbacks as Opportunities for Growth Turning Life's Lemons into a Whole Spiritual Lemonade Stand 16

Chapter 5
Developing Resilience and Emotional Strength Bouncing Back Stronger—One Setback at a Time 21

Chapter 6
Discovering Purpose Through Pain Turning Life's Rough Patches into Roadmaps to Your Calling 26

Chapter 7
Building a Personal Spiritual Healing Practice Creating a Daily Routine for Growth, Grounding, and Inner Peace 31

Chapter 8
Healing Past Wounds and Breaking Patterns Letting Go of the Past and Setting Yourself Free.. 37

Chapter 9
Soul Growth Through Self-Love and Empowerment Building a Foundation of Compassion, Confidence, and True Strength 42

Chapter 10
Embracing Gratitude and Finding Joy Amid Setbacks Celebrating Life's Small Moments to Fuel Healing and Growth... 48

Chapter 11
Moving Forward: Integrating Growth and Embracing the Journey Living with Purpose, Confidence, and an Open Heart 53

Chapter 12
Embracing Your Power and Living Fully Stepping into Your Authentic Self and Creating a Life You Love... 58

Conclusion
A Journey Well Traveled, A Life Ready to Be Lived 62

Appendix
Resources for Continued Growth and Healing 63

Introduction

From Rock Bottom to Rising Strong

My journey to healing and self-discovery wasn't smooth, pretty, or wrapped in a bow. It was raw, messy, and deeply personal—a journey born from rock-bottom moments, times when I felt trapped in cycles of pain, shame, and self-doubt. I didn't begin this path with a clear map or even a sense of direction. I started it because I had to, because life had brought me to a breaking point and I realized I needed something more than survival. I needed purpose, growth, and a way to find peace within myself.

For years, I carried the weight of my past—a past filled with addiction, trauma, and painful truths I could barely face. From a young age, I experienced abuse and rejection that left scars far deeper than I knew at the time. The pain shaped me in ways I didn't fully understand; it affected my relationships, led me down roads of self-destruction, and clouded my sense of self-worth. By my twenties, I was lost in addiction, seeking an escape from emotions that felt too big to handle. I buried myself in substances, hoping to numb the ache that echoed through every part of me. The turning point came at a dark moment when I found myself alone, staring at the consequences of a lifetime of unresolved pain.

But rock bottom became my foundation. It was the place where I finally decided to look within, to peel back the layers of hurt, and to confront the parts of myself I'd been avoiding for so long. It wasn't easy. Healing never is. It's not about following a straight path to enlightenment or ticking boxes on a checklist. It's stumbling, falling, getting up again, and finding the courage to face yourself, scars and all. But as I slowly began to let go of the past, to forgive myself for the choices I made in my darkest hours, and to truly understand what self-love means, I discovered a strength I didn't know I had. I learned that healing isn't about erasing the scars; it's about transforming them into sources of wisdom, resilience, and compassion.

This book is a guide for those who find themselves in dark places, who feel burdened by the weight of the past, or who are simply seeking a deeper sense of purpose and peace. It's filled with the insights, tools, and practices that helped me on my path, shared with the hope that they'll help you on yours. My journey is not unique, and I know there are others out there who have walked similar paths, who've experienced rock-bottom moments, and who are ready to start rising again. Whether you're just beginning your healing journey or are well on your way, know that every step matters. There's strength in your struggle, and there's power in your story. You're not alone on this path; we're all walking it together, each of us learning, healing, and growing along the way.

Thank you for allowing me to share this journey with you. I hope these pages serve as a reminder that no matter how deep the pain, there is always a way forward—a way to transform, heal, and become unbreakable. This book is my story, but it's also yours. Together, let's walk this path to healing, resilience, and the life you truly deserve.

Chapter 1

Understanding Spiritual Healing and Soul Growth
Turning Life's Curveballs into Cosmic Growth Opportunities

Let's be real: Life sometimes throws us curveballs, and not the fun kind you catch with a glove and a cheer. No, life's curveballs can knock us flat, leave us seeing stars, and wondering, "Why me?" But what if, instead of staying face-down on the field, we saw those moments as spiritual plot twists? Believe it or not, those messy, painful, seriously-how-did-this-happen-to-me moments can be the start of something beautiful. And that, my friend, is the essence of spiritual healing and soul growth.

What Is Spiritual Healing Anyway?

Think of spiritual healing as the ultimate spa day for your soul. We're talking about cleansing the emotional toxins, soaking away past hurts, and emerging refreshed and realigned. Unlike a spa day, though, it's not a one-and-done thing. It's a journey. And yes, sometimes it's a journey that feels like you're wearing heels in quicksand.

Spiritual healing is about peeling back the layers of pain, fear, and conditioning that keep us from feeling whole. It's about gently (or not-so-gently) letting go of what doesn't serve us, whether that's an ancient grudge or a self-doubt that's been hanging out rent-free in your mind. It's about finding inner peace, not by pretending everything is rainbows and unicorns, but by accepting the storms as part of the scenery.

You don't have to have it all figured out to start healing. In fact, most people begin without a clue of what they're doing (or why). Healing is less about knowing the steps and more about being willing to take them, even if that means stumbling a bit. The path might not look like you imagined, but trust that every awkward, wobbly step is getting you closer to who you're meant to be.

And Soul Growth? That Sounds Important.

You bet it is. Soul growth is like leveling up in the game of life. Picture your soul as a garden that, with each challenge, either wilts or blooms. Each setback is a new seed, and every lesson learned is like miracle grow for your spirit. Soul growth means evolving, expanding, and (hopefully) outgrowing those limiting beliefs and self-sabotaging habits that used to keep you boxed in.

But here's the thing: Soul growth doesn't happen on its own. It's not just something that happens because you're aging (although, fingers crossed, that helps). Soul growth happens because you roll up your sleeves, get a little dirt under your nails, and decide to turn your life's compost into fertile ground.

Growth isn't glamorous; it's gritty, awkward, and humbling. It's late-night soul-searching, unexpected realizations, and the kind of change that makes you look back and say, "Wow, I can't believe I made it through that." And as you grow, you realize it's not about reaching some finish line but about becoming more aligned with who you truly are.

Setbacks as Secret Ingredients

I know, I know, hearing "setbacks are opportunities" can feel like someone telling you kale is a "treat." But the truth is, those tough moments are like hidden treasure chests waiting to be cracked open. In the world of soul growth, setbacks are often the keys that unlock our next level. Each challenge, from the embarrassing to the epic, is a chance to learn something new about yourself and the world. Think of it this way: Setbacks are just "soul vitamins." A bit hard to swallow, but boy, do they boost your spiritual immune system.

There's a weird magic to embracing setbacks. When you start seeing them as part of the plan (even if it's a plan that feels like it's written in hieroglyphics), you realize each low point was a setup for a breakthrough. Your soul begins to trust the process, and you discover the power of resilience.

Reimagining the Path: From Victim to Victor

This part might be the trickiest. It's tempting to play the "Why me?" card—and hey, we've all been there. But here's the twist: What if, instead of seeing life as a series of unfortunate events happening to you, you saw it as a grand cosmic boot camp designed for you? What if each setback was actually life's weirdly wonderful way of saying, "Hey, you're stronger than you think?"

Moving from victim to victor isn't about pretending everything's fine when it's clearly not. It's about taking back the pen and deciding how this chapter of your story is going to end. Spoiler alert: It's going to be epic, and you're going to be the hero.

Stepping into the role of victor requires courage, vulnerability, and a willingness to rewrite the narrative. It's about recognizing that while you may not control every twist and turn, you can control your response. And in that choice, you reclaim your power.

Embracing the Messy Journey

Here's the thing: Spiritual healing and soul growth are messy. They don't come with step-by-step instructions or guaranteed outcomes. Sometimes, they don't even come with good explanations! But if you're willing to embrace the mess, if you're willing to get curious about what each struggle is trying to teach you, you might just find that life's curveballs have a strange way of pointing you toward something better.

This journey isn't about perfection; it's about progress. It's about choosing to show up for yourself, even when it's hard, even when you'd rather pull the covers over your head. So grab a journal, light a candle, or maybe just sit quietly with your morning coffee. Give yourself permission to feel, to forgive, and to imagine new possibilities. This is the start of something bigger than the setbacks. This is the beginning of turning life's curveballs into cosmic blessings. And trust me, it's a journey worth taking.

Take a deep breath. You're exactly where you need to be. Remember, this journey is uniquely yours, but you're not alone. In the next chapter, we're diving into the art of letting go (and yes, it's way harder than it sounds). But for now, just breathe, reflect, and trust the process. You've got this.

Chapter 2

The Healing Process – Accepting, Acknowledging, and Letting Go
Or, How to Release the Baggage Without Booking a One-Way Ticket to Nowhere

Alright, so you've decided to go on this spiritual healing journey. Bravo! That's half the battle. Now comes the part where we really roll up our sleeves and dig into what I like to call "the messy middle"—where we learn to accept, acknowledge, and (gulp) let go. Yes, these are the biggies of the healing process. But don't worry, I'll be here to help you navigate each step, and maybe we'll even laugh a little along the way.

Step One: Accepting Reality (a.k.a. Letting Go of Fantasy Island)

Acceptance is the bedrock of healing, but let's face it—it's also the hardest. Accepting reality means coming to terms with things as they are, not as we wish they could be. It's the moment we say, "Yep, that happened. That's my story, messy parts and all." And I won't lie to you; it can feel a little bit like swallowing a cactus.

But acceptance isn't about giving up or admitting defeat. No, acceptance is actually about freeing up all that mental and emotional energy you've been wasting on "should haves" and "could haves." When we accept what's happened, we're no longer wrestling with reality. We're stepping into it, owning it, and, ultimately, moving forward from it.

It's easy to get stuck fantasizing about how things "should have" been different. But every time we cling to these "shoulds," we're denying ourselves the chance to make peace with the present. So here's an exercise to start accepting: Sit down with a journal (or a napkin, or the back of an envelope—whatever you have handy) and write down the things you've been fighting to accept. No sugarcoating, no editing—just the raw, real deal. Look at what you've written. Take a deep breath, and repeat after me: "This happened. And I can still be okay."

Step Two: Acknowledging the Pain Without Pitching a Tent in It

Acceptance is about seeing reality, but acknowledgment is about feeling it. Yes, I know, this one sounds even scarier. But hear me out. If we don't acknowledge the feelings tied to our experiences—the sadness, the anger, the disappointment—those emotions just stay bottled up, popping out at the worst possible times (think: tear-filled rants over spilled coffee or existential crises in the grocery store).

Acknowledgment doesn't mean wallowing. It's simply allowing yourself to feel the feels, to let the emotions flow without judgment. It's a bit like giving your feelings a seat at the table instead of shoving them in the broom closet. This part is all about creating space for your emotions, letting them have their moment without letting them move in permanently.

One trick I love for this is a quick emotion check-in. Set a timer for five minutes, sit quietly, and ask yourself: "What am I feeling right now?" Don't analyze, don't fix. Just notice. You might be surprised what bubbles up. And the beautiful thing? When we let emotions rise and acknowledge them, they tend to soften all on their own.

Step Three: Letting Go (Cue the Deep Sigh of Relief)

Letting go is the grand finale, the part where we release the weight of past hurts, regrets, and all those "what ifs." But contrary to popular belief, letting go isn't about forgetting or pretending it didn't happen. Letting go means we're ready to move forward without dragging our emotional baggage behind us like some sort of tragic, cosmic ball and chain.

Now, let's be honest—sometimes letting go feels like losing a part of ourselves. We get attached to our stories, even the painful ones, because they've shaped who we are. But true letting go is about honoring the past without letting it define your future. It's a conscious decision to put down the weight and say, "I am more than my past."

For a simple letting-go practice, try this: Write a letter to the person, situation, or feeling you're ready to release. Spill it all. Then, when you're done, read it over, thank it for whatever it taught you (even if that lesson was, "Never again!"), and either tear it up, burn it (safely, please), or bury it. There's something incredibly freeing about physically releasing the words you've been holding onto.

Bonus Step: Finding the Humor in the Healing

Look, the healing process can be heavy, but don't forget to laugh along the way. Humor is one of the greatest healing tools we have. When we can look at our struggles with a bit of levity, they lose some of their power over us. I'm not saying every moment is funny, but sometimes, a bit of well-placed humor is exactly what we need to lighten the load.

Try this: When you're deep in the process of letting go, think about how you'd describe this moment in a comedy. Imagine telling your story to a close friend who just gets you. You might find that what felt so overwhelming a minute ago starts to look, well, a little ridiculous (in the best possible way).

Embracing the Process: The Art of Patience with Yourself

Healing isn't a race. It's not something you check off your to-do list. It's a winding, twisting journey with highs, lows, and some weird detours along the way. And here's the most important part: Be patient with yourself. Some days, you'll feel like you're moving mountains. Other days, getting out of bed might feel like the victory. Both are okay.

Healing doesn't happen overnight. There will be days where you feel on top of the world and others where you feel like you're back at square one. That's the nature of the process. Give yourself grace. Healing takes time, and that's perfectly normal. The goal isn't to "get over it" but to get through it in your own time, at your own pace.

A Note on Self-Compassion

As you move through the steps of acceptance, acknowledgment, and letting go, remember to be kind to yourself. The journey isn't linear, and there are no shortcuts. Self-compassion is the glue that holds the process together. Every time you stumble, forgive yourself. Every time you make progress, celebrate it. Healing is in each moment you choose to release, forgive, and let life flow.

So, there you have it: Accept, acknowledge, and let go. Remember, this journey isn't about perfection; it's about progress. And even on those days when progress feels as slow as a snail on a stroll, remember that every step you take is a step forward. Healing isn't just something you do—it's something you become. It's in each moment you choose to release, forgive, and let life flow.

Chapter 3

Self-Reflection and Inner Awareness
Becoming Your Own Best Detective (Without the Trench Coat and Magnifying Glass)

Alright, so you've tackled acceptance, you've had a good look at your emotions, and maybe even let go of a few of those dusty old grievances. Now it's time to dive a little deeper. This is where we get curious, where we really start to unravel the mystery of you. Welcome to the world of self-reflection and inner awareness—a place where we ask the big questions, listen carefully to the answers, and maybe find a few surprises along the way.

Why Self-Reflection Is Key to Soul Growth

Think of self-reflection as a mirror for your inner life. Just like you'd check a mirror to see if you have spinach in your teeth before a big meeting, self-reflection helps you check for those less-visible things hanging out in your mind and heart. It's about noticing the beliefs, fears, and dreams that guide (or misguide) us. And here's the kicker: the more we see ourselves clearly, the better we can understand why we do what we do—and make choices that actually serve us instead of tripping us up.

So, why bother with self-reflection? Because awareness is where real change begins. When we see ourselves honestly, we can start to shed old patterns, embrace our strengths, and grow in ways we didn't think possible. And who doesn't want to feel like they've got life a little more figured out?

Self-reflection gives us the power to stop running on autopilot. Instead of simply reacting to life, we can respond intentionally. This process invites us to dive beneath the surface, beyond the quick fixes and shallow solutions, and to truly understand what's driving us.

Techniques for Deep Self-Reflection: Going Beyond Surface Level

Self-reflection isn't just staring at a blank wall and waiting for life-changing revelations (though, hey, stranger things have happened). It's a practice, and like any good practice, it takes a little technique. Here are a few tools to help you get started:

1. **The Journal of Truth** Grab a notebook and a pen and let's get real. Journaling is one of the most powerful ways to dig into your inner world. But instead of "Dear Diary" entries, we're talking raw, unfiltered honesty. Ask yourself questions like:

    - What do I fear the most right now?
    - Where am I holding back in life?
    - What does my heart truly want, and what's standing in the way?

    Write without censoring. Let it all out, even the parts that make you cringe. This is for your eyes only, so be bold, be messy, and watch as new insights emerge from the pages.

2. **Meditation with a Twist** Meditation isn't just for chilling out (though that's a nice bonus). It's also a powerful tool for observing yourself without judgment. Try this: Set a timer for five minutes, close your eyes, and focus on your breath. Each time a thought pops up, instead of pushing it away, just notice it. Is it anxious? Excited? Negative? This simple act of observation helps you see your thoughts for what they are—just thoughts, not absolute truths. Over time, this practice helps you detach from old patterns and beliefs.

3. **Talking to Your Inner Child (Yes, Really)** Sometimes, the things that hold us back the most are beliefs we've carried around since we were little. This technique might sound a bit woo-woo, but stay with me—it can be

surprisingly powerful. Close your eyes, imagine yourself as a child, and ask them how they're feeling. What are they afraid of? What do they need? Listen carefully to the answers. You might just find that some of the patterns you're trying to break started years ago—and that by showing compassion to that "inner kid," you can finally start to let those patterns go.

Identifying Patterns and Limiting Beliefs: Spotting the Usual Suspects

Now that you're diving deep, it's time to become a bit of a detective. Everyone has patterns—those pesky habits or beliefs that keep popping up and throwing a wrench in our plans. Maybe it's self-doubt, a fear of failure, or a need to control everything (hey, no judgment). The key is to recognize these patterns for what they are: old scripts that don't actually define you.

Take some time to notice when these thoughts or behaviors appear. Is there a common trigger? How does it make you feel? The more you can see these patterns for what they are—unhelpful habits rather than facts about yourself—the more power you have to choose a new way forward.

Here's a quick exercise to try: The next time you feel a limiting belief creeping in (like "I'm not good enough" or "I'll never figure this out"), stop and say, "Is that really true?" Just questioning it can help loosen its grip on you. Over time, you'll start to notice these beliefs losing their power, and a new, more empowered perspective taking their place.

Recognizing the Role of Ego vs. Intuition

Ah, the ego—always ready to jump in with opinions, fears, and judgments. Our ego often thinks it's protecting us, but it's mostly just loud and a bit dramatic. Intuition, on the other hand, is quieter. It's that deep, calm voice that doesn't shout but nudges us gently in the right direction.

Learning to tell the difference between ego and intuition is a huge part of self-awareness. Ego usually feels urgent, loud, and maybe a bit judgmental. Intuition feels calm, wise, and steady. When you feel stuck in a decision, ask yourself: Am I listening to my ego, or is this truly my intuition speaking?

One way to strengthen your connection to intuition is through regular quiet time—whether that's meditation, nature walks, or even just a few moments of stillness each day. The more you listen, the easier it is to distinguish between the two. Trusting your intuition can feel strange at first, but as you practice, it becomes a guiding light in your journey.

Getting Curious, Not Critical

As you go through this process, it's easy to get a bit judgy with yourself. You might find yourself thinking, "Why did I do that?" or "I should be better at this by now." But here's a radical thought: what if you approached self-reflection with curiosity instead of criticism? Imagine you're a kind-hearted detective, examining clues, not assigning blame.

Try this: The next time you catch yourself in an old pattern, don't beat yourself up. Just ask, "Huh, that's interesting. I wonder where that came from?" This simple shift in perspective can make a huge difference. Self-discovery should feel like peeling back layers, not chipping away at your own self-worth.

Celebrating the Little Wins

Self-reflection and inner awareness aren't just about digging up every flaw or fixing every mistake. They're also about celebrating the progress you make along the way. Maybe you're catching yourself in a limiting belief a little quicker. Or maybe you're noticing moments when your intuition speaks up. These are wins, and they deserve to be celebrated. After all, soul growth isn't a sprint—it's a lifelong marathon, and every step forward matters.

Embracing the Journey: Being Open to What You Find

In self-reflection, there will be moments of clarity, times of discomfort, and some discoveries that surprise you. Be open to all of it. Each insight, each new layer uncovered, brings you closer to understanding yourself fully. This journey isn't about fixing or perfecting yourself; it's about embracing all of who you are—every flaw, every strength, and every lesson learned along the way.

So there you have it: The art of self-reflection. It's about noticing, getting curious, and maybe even laughing at the parts of yourself that are a little ridiculous (don't worry, we all have them). Remember, this isn't about perfection—it's about exploration, and there's no wrong way to do it.

In the next chapter, we'll start diving into the real magic: reframing setbacks as growth opportunities. So grab your journal, a warm drink, and get ready to keep unraveling the mystery of you. Who knows what you'll discover?

Chapter 4

Reframing Setbacks as Opportunities for Growth
Turning Life's Lemons into a Whole Spiritual Lemonade Stand

Setbacks are part of life. They show up uninvited, just when you're getting comfortable. Whether it's heartbreak, job loss, rejection, or just a canceled plan, these curveballs have a knack for throwing us off balance. But what if, instead of seeing setbacks as cosmic punishments, we started seeing them as invitations? Invitations to grow, learn, and transform in ways we might never have expected.

Reframing setbacks as growth opportunities doesn't mean pretending everything is fine. It means choosing to see the potential for growth in even the messiest situations. It's about saying, "Okay, this isn't what I planned, but maybe there's something here for me." Let's dig into the art of reframing and start turning life's challenges into stepping stones.

The Power of Perspective: Why Reframing Matters

Reframing is about shifting your perspective. Imagine your mind as a camera, and each setback is like a snapshot. Right now, you might be zoomed in on the difficulty, the disappointment, the pain. But what if you zoomed out? What if you looked at the situation from a different angle? Changing the way we view setbacks can help us see beyond the immediate challenge and recognize the potential for growth.

Our mindset shapes how we experience life. When we choose to reframe, we're not ignoring the hard stuff; we're choosing to see beyond it. We're saying, "Yes, this is difficult, but maybe there's something valuable here, something that could make me stronger, wiser, or more resilient." By changing our perspective, we transform setbacks from obstacles into stepping stones that move us forward on our journey.

The magic of reframing is that it empowers us. Instead of feeling like life is happening *to* us, we start to see that it's happening *for* us. Every challenge, every disappointment, is an opportunity to grow, to adapt, and to become a little bit more of who we're meant to be.

Reframing in Action: Practical Steps to Shift Your Perspective

Reframing doesn't happen automatically—it's a choice we make. Here are some ways to get started:

1. **Ask, "What Can I Learn from This?"** Every setback, no matter how frustrating, carries a lesson. It could be teaching you patience, resilience, or helping you clarify what you truly want. When life throws a challenge your way, pause and ask, "What can I learn from this?" Sometimes the lesson isn't immediately obvious, but by asking the question, you open yourself up to new insights.

    Try this: Write down three possible lessons you could learn from a current setback. You might find that it's nudging you toward a new path or teaching you something valuable about yourself.

2. **Look for the Silver Lining (Yes, They Exist!)** Even in tough times, there's often something positive—whether it's a skill you gained, a deeper relationship, or a newfound strength. Finding the silver lining isn't about minimizing your experience; it's about noticing the good that can come from it.

    When faced with a setback, jot down a few positive outcomes that could arise. Maybe a job loss gives you time to pursue a passion project, or a breakup allows you to grow in self-love. These little glimpses of light can help you keep moving forward, even when things feel heavy.

3. **Reframe Your Language** The words we use shape our reality. If you keep telling yourself, "This is a disaster," it's going to feel pretty miserable. But if you reframe it with words like, "This is challenging, but I'm learning

from it," or "This is helping me grow," it can make the situation feel a bit more manageable.

Language is powerful, so choose words that empower rather than drag you down. Turn your self-talk into a pep talk. You'll be amazed at how much your perspective can shift with a few changes in phrasing. Start to speak to yourself the way you would to a friend—kindly, encouragingly, and with an understanding that setbacks don't define you.

4. **Focus on What You Can Control** The worst part of setbacks is often the feeling of losing control. Reframing involves focusing on what you *can* control instead of what you can't. You can't change the past, but you can control how you respond in the present. Ask yourself, "What's one small thing I can do right now?" Maybe it's taking a deep breath, making a plan, or reaching out for support. By focusing on what's within your power, setbacks start to feel less overwhelming. By shifting your focus to what you can do, you regain a sense of agency. This simple action grounds you in the present moment and reminds you that, no matter the challenge, you have the ability to shape your next step.

From "Why Me?" to "What's Next?"

It's normal to ask "Why me?" when life throws a tough situation your way. But staying in that mindset keeps you feeling stuck. Reframing means shifting from "Why is this happening to me?" to "What can I do with this?" or "What's next for me?" This small shift can make a big difference.

Try this: The next time you find yourself in "Why me?" mode, pause and reframe it to "What's next?" This language shift moves you out of helplessness and into action, opening the door to growth. It's a reminder that you're not defined by your setbacks, but by how you rise above them.

Real-Life Examples of Reframing

Let's look at a few scenarios to see how reframing can change our experience of setbacks:

- **Lost a Job?** Instead of seeing it as a failure, view it as a chance to explore new opportunities, build new skills, or finally start that passion project you've been dreaming about.

- **Going Through a Breakup?** Rather than focusing on the loss, consider it as an opportunity to redefine what you want in relationships, deepen self-love, and reconnect with yourself.

- **Missed Opportunity?** Instead of feeling regret, remind yourself that sometimes things don't work out because something better is on the horizon.

Each of these scenarios can be painful, but reframing helps us move beyond the immediate hurt and see the potential for something more. In the long run, these reframed setbacks often lead us to experiences and people we never would have encountered otherwise.

Embracing Setbacks as Part of the Journey

The journey of soul growth is rarely straightforward. It's filled with unexpected detours, wrong turns, and the occasional pitstop in "What-Am-I-Doing-With-My-Life" town. But here's the truth: setbacks are part of the process. They're not roadblocks; they're the raw materials that help us build resilience, perspective, and strength.

Remember, reframing setbacks doesn't mean you have to love them. You don't have to be grateful for every disappointment. But by choosing to see them as opportunities for growth, you're giving yourself the chance to transform those experiences into something meaningful. You're turning the bitter lemons of life into something that fuels your journey.

Setbacks don't define us; they refine us. They push us to stretch beyond our comfort zones and discover strengths we didn't know we had. By embracing these challenges, we're allowing ourselves to grow in unexpected ways and preparing for a future that's richer and more resilient.

So, here's your mission: Start looking at your challenges through a different lens. When life hands you a setback, ask yourself, "How can this help me grow?" You may not have all the answers right away, and that's okay. Soul growth is a slow, steady climb, but with every step, you're moving forward.

In the next chapter, we'll dive into resilience and how to build emotional strength for the journey ahead. Because as you'll soon discover, setbacks don't stand a chance against a resilient heart.

Chapter 5

Developing Resilience and Emotional Strength
Bouncing Back Stronger—One Setback at a Time

When life throws us curveballs, it's easy to want to duck and cover. But here's the thing: resilience isn't about avoiding the tough stuff. It's about standing up, facing it, and saying, "Is that all you've got?" And let's be real—resilience is a skill forged in the fires of real challenges, not something that just magically appears. If there's one thing I've learned, it's that resilience grows from facing down the shadows and coming back stronger, even if you're a little bruised.

In this chapter, we're diving into the art of resilience, from how to find your footing when things feel shaky to building emotional strength that will keep you steady, no matter what storms roll in.

Resilience: What It Is (and What It Isn't)

Let's start with what resilience isn't. It isn't pretending everything is fine, bottling up your emotions, or pushing yourself to "just get over it." True resilience is about facing your emotions head-on, honoring them, and learning how to move through them. It's about finding strength in the struggle, not in ignoring it.

Resilience doesn't mean you don't get knocked down. It means that when you do, you get back up—again and again. It's about being able to say, "Yes, this happened, but it's not going to break me." And trust me, I've been through enough to know that this mindset doesn't come overnight. Building resilience is a journey, one that requires patience, self-compassion, and a willingness to keep moving forward, even when it's hard.

True resilience is about learning to navigate the ups and downs with a steady heart, knowing that every setback is an opportunity to build strength, patience, and emotional fortitude.

Lessons from Rock Bottom: How Hitting Low Points Builds Resilience

I've had my share of low points—the kind that leave you staring at the ceiling, wondering how you're ever going to put the pieces back together. For me, one of those rock-bottom moments came when I found myself in a dark place, grappling with addiction, trauma, and self-doubt. At 27, I was facing demons I'd buried for years, struggling to cope with a past that included early abuse, addiction, and deep-rooted pain.

When you hit rock bottom, it can feel like there's no way out. But if I've learned anything from those dark nights, it's that rock bottom can also be a turning point. It can be the place where you make the decision to rise. Rock bottom, painful as it is, strips away everything superficial. It leaves you with the raw, unfiltered truth of who you are—and who you can become.

Rock bottom isn't a place anyone wants to be, but it's a place of profound clarity. When everything falls apart, you're left with the foundation, the core of who you are. And from that place, you have the chance to rebuild, stronger and wiser than before.

Building Resilience: Practical Steps for Emotional Strength

So, how do we actually build resilience? It's one thing to talk about being strong, but let's get practical. Here are some steps that helped me, and that might help you when you're ready to stand back up, stronger than before.

1. **Embrace Vulnerability (Yes, Even When It's Terrifying)** Resilience begins with vulnerability. When you let yourself feel what you need to feel—anger, sadness, frustration—you start to process it instead of letting it fester. Vulnerability isn't weakness; it's courage. It's saying, "This hurts, but I'm going to face it."

I had to learn this the hard way. For years, I kept my emotions bottled up, trying to pretend that everything was fine when it wasn't. But once I allowed myself to be vulnerable, to let those close to me see my scars and struggles, I found a strength I didn't know I had. Sharing your story, or even just admitting your own pain to yourself, is an act of resilience.

2. **Develop a Daily Practice for Self-Reflection** Resilience isn't built overnight—it's a daily practice. One way to strengthen your emotional foundation is through regular self-reflection. Set aside a few minutes each day to check in with yourself. How are you feeling? What's weighing on your heart? What small step can you take to address it?

   Journaling was a lifeline for me. It helped me get my thoughts out of my head and onto paper, where I could start to make sense of them. Journaling doesn't have to be fancy or poetic; it's just about putting your feelings down in a place where they can breathe. Self-reflection lets you track your progress and notice patterns, so you can keep moving forward, even if it's just one step at a time.

3. **Cultivate Self-Compassion (Especially on the Hard Days)** When you're on a journey of healing, you're going to stumble. There are going to be days when you feel like you've taken three steps forward and two steps back. In those moments, self-compassion is essential. Be gentle with yourself. Remember that healing isn't linear, and growth doesn't happen without setbacks.

   For years, I beat myself up over every mistake, every relapse, every time I didn't live up to my own standards. But self-compassion means treating yourself like a friend. It's acknowledging that you're doing the best you can with what you have. And on the hardest days, it's reminding yourself that setbacks don't erase your progress.

4. **Lean on a Support System** Resilience doesn't mean doing it all alone. Leaning on a support system is one of the best ways to build strength. Whether it's family, friends, or a trusted mentor, having people who can lift you up and remind you of your worth is invaluable. I wouldn't be

where I am today without the support of those who stood by me through the hardest times.

There was a time when I felt ashamed to ask for help. But resilience is knowing when you need others. It's about reaching out when you're struggling and letting people support you on the journey. The truth is, we're stronger together. Your support system can offer perspective, encouragement, and sometimes just a safe space to cry it out.

5. **Set Small Goals and Celebrate Small Wins** When you're facing a setback, it's easy to feel overwhelmed by the mountain ahead of you. That's why setting small, achievable goals can make all the difference. Each small win builds confidence and reminds you that you're moving forward, even if it doesn't feel like it at first.

   When I was clawing my way back from rock bottom, I started small—sometimes my only goal was just to get through the day without falling back into old habits. But each small win, each day I stayed sober, each moment I chose self-care, built resilience. These wins add up, so celebrate them. Don't wait for the big victory to pat yourself on the back—acknowledge the little steps that are moving you forward.

6. **Create a Mindfulness Practice to Stay Grounded** Resilience grows when we're grounded, when we're connected to the present moment rather than caught up in fears about the future or regrets from the past. Practicing mindfulness, whether it's through meditation, breathwork, or just spending a few moments in nature, helps to anchor you.

   Mindfulness was one of the tools that helped me stay present during tough times. When you're able to slow down, to notice your breath and your surroundings, it's easier to handle whatever life throws at you. Mindfulness reminds you that you're more than your past, more than your mistakes, and that in this moment, you're okay.

Resilience in Action: Taking Your Power Back

Resilience isn't just about bouncing back; it's about taking your power back. It's about facing those parts of yourself that you might have avoided, the old wounds, the buried memories, the hidden fears. It's about saying, "I'm in control of my story, and I get to choose how it ends."

Each step you take in building resilience strengthens you. It brings you closer to that unshakable part of yourself that can weather any storm. It's a journey, but one that transforms you, making you more compassionate, more courageous, and more connected to your true self.

Embracing Your Strength

Remember, resilience doesn't mean you won't feel pain. It means you'll find strength in the pain. It means you'll learn, grow, and transform, turning life's toughest moments into sources of power. This journey isn't about "bouncing back"—it's about bouncing forward, carrying with you the lessons, strength, and courage you've gained along the way.

In the next chapter, we'll dive into discovering your purpose through pain and learning how life's challenges can guide you toward your true calling.

Chapter 6

Discovering Purpose Through Pain
Turning Life's Rough Patches into Roadmaps to Your Calling

*I*f life were easy, we'd all have a clear path, free of twists, turns, and roadblocks. But, as we know, life isn't a smooth highway. It's more like a winding trail full of unexpected bumps, detours, and, sometimes, landslides. But here's the thing—often, those very obstacles are what guide us to our purpose. In fact, if you're paying attention, your toughest moments might just be trying to tell you something about who you really are and why you're here.

Pain, heartbreak, loss, and setbacks all have a way of stripping us down, taking away our illusions, and leaving us with the core of who we are. And while none of us would willingly sign up for suffering, the truth is that pain often becomes the portal to discovering what truly matters. In this chapter, we're exploring how life's challenges can illuminate our purpose and guide us toward a deeper, more meaningful path.

Why Pain and Purpose Are Often Partners

It may sound like a cruel twist of fate, but pain and purpose often go hand in hand. Pain has a way of waking us up, of shattering the things we thought we knew and forcing us to look deeper. When everything else falls away, we're left with the truth of who we are and what we value. And sometimes, that truth points us directly toward our purpose.

When I look back at my own journey—through addiction, trauma, and dark times—I can see how each painful experience pushed me closer to my calling. My struggles weren't just random events; they were the very things that led me to a place of understanding, empathy, and a desire to help others on their journey.

Each piece of pain became a piece of the puzzle, showing me what I was meant to do.

Pain has a unique way of clarifying what's important. It strips away the superficial and brings us face-to-face with our core values. Often, it's in the moments when we feel broken that we uncover what truly makes us whole.

Signs That Pain Is Pointing You Toward Your Purpose

Not all painful experiences will lead to a grand "aha!" moment, but often, there are clues hiding within the struggle. Here are some signs that a painful experience might be nudging you toward your purpose:

1. **You Feel a Strong Urge to Help Others in Similar Situations** When you've gone through something intense, there's often a deep, instinctual pull to help others facing the same thing. If you've survived something, you now have insight and empathy that others need. This doesn't mean you need to make it your career, but following that urge can bring you closer to a sense of purpose.

2. **Your Pain Transforms into Passion** Sometimes, a painful experience fuels a passion that wasn't there before. Maybe a health scare leads you to a calling in wellness, or heartbreak ignites a desire to empower others in self-love. Pay attention to where your interests shift after a struggle—these new passions might just be pointing you toward your purpose.

3. **You Find Meaning or Lessons That You Want to Share** When you find yourself reflecting on a painful experience and seeing valuable lessons within it, you're already on the path to transformation. Sharing those insights, whether through writing, speaking, teaching, or simply being there for others, can be a powerful way to bring purpose to your pain.

Painful experiences can often reveal passions, insights, and strengths that were dormant within us. They help us identify what we truly care about and what we feel driven to share with the world.

Turning Pain into Purpose: Practical Steps

Transforming pain into purpose isn't about forcing yourself to "get over it" or pretending everything is fine. It's about honoring the experience, finding meaning in it, and then channeling that meaning into something greater. Here are some practical ways to start turning your pain into purpose:

1. **Reflect on Your Hardest Experiences and What They've Taught You**: Begin by looking back on some of your toughest moments. What did those experiences teach you about yourself, about others, about life? This isn't about romanticizing the pain—it's about recognizing the strength, insight, or wisdom you gained from it.

    Try this: Make a list of three to five significant challenges you've faced and, next to each one, write down at least one thing you learned from it. Maybe you discovered resilience, compassion, or a new perspective. Each lesson is a piece of your purpose puzzle.

2. **Ask Yourself, "Who Can I Help with What I've Learned?"**: If you've gone through something difficult, chances are there are others going through the same thing. Consider how you might use your experience to support, inspire, or uplift others. You don't have to start a nonprofit or make a grand gesture—sometimes just sharing your story, offering a listening ear, or giving advice to a friend can be enough.

    There's power in saying, "I've been where you are, and I understand." Sometimes, our purpose is simply to be a light for someone still walking through the darkness we once faced.

3. **Take Action, No Matter How Small**: Purpose isn't always a big, glamorous thing. Sometimes, it's as simple as taking small steps to make a difference. Maybe it's starting a blog, volunteering, taking a course that interests you, or writing down your story. Action transforms pain into purpose, one small step at a time.

    When I began my journey of helping others, it didn't start with a grand plan. It began with one-on-one conversations, with being vulnerable enough to share my story. Each action, no matter how small, helped me shape my purpose.

4. **Be Open to Redefining What "Purpose" Means to You:** It's easy to feel like "purpose" has to be a fixed, one-size-fits-all mission. But purpose is personal, and it changes as we grow. Sometimes, it's about being a good friend, sometimes it's sharing your talents, and sometimes it's just being there for yourself. Let your purpose be flexible, adaptable, and something that evolves with you.

For me, purpose has been a journey. It started as a quest to heal myself, then it grew into a desire to help others heal, and now, it's become something bigger—something that keeps evolving as I do. Be open to the possibility that your purpose can change over time, and that's okay.

Finding Joy and Gratitude in the Journey

As you turn your pain into purpose, remember to find joy along the way. Life's journey, even with all its ups and downs, is something to celebrate. Find moments of gratitude, whether it's for the strength you've gained, the people who've supported you, or the insights you've uncovered. Purpose isn't just about a destination; it's about the way we walk the path.

Practicing gratitude can help shift your focus from what you've lost to what you've gained. It reminds you that even in the most challenging times, there are things worth celebrating—like the courage it takes to keep moving forward, the wisdom that pain has given you, and the ways your life can inspire others.

Embracing Your Purpose as Part of Your Story

Remember, purpose doesn't have to be something grand or world-changing. Sometimes, it's just about showing up as the best version of yourself. Embracing your purpose is about honoring your journey, trusting that your experiences—especially the tough ones—have value, and believing that you're here for a reason.

Your journey, with all its twists, turns, and hard-won lessons, has brought you to this point. Embrace it. Use it. Let your purpose be a light, not only for others but for yourself. This is how we take what life gives us and turn it into something meaningful, something that not only heals us but also has the potential to heal others.

In the next chapter, we'll look at building a personal spiritual healing practice that keeps you grounded, connected, and ready to continue your journey, whatever comes next.

Chapter 7

Building a Personal Spiritual Healing Practice
Creating a Daily Routine for Growth, Grounding, and Inner Peace

Congratulations, my friend. You've journeyed through some heavy, transformative chapters, and you're starting to see the purpose and power in your story. Now, it's time to turn all that insight and resilience into a daily practice that keeps you grounded, connected, and growing. Think of this chapter as your guide to building a spiritual healing routine—a personalized toolkit you can rely on every day, no matter what life throws your way.

A spiritual healing practice doesn't need to be complicated or time-consuming. It's about creating habits and rituals that remind you of who you are, help you stay centered, and make space for continued growth. Let's dive into how you can create a meaningful, sustainable daily practice that feels like a gift to your spirit.

Why a Daily Spiritual Practice Matters

Having a daily practice is like giving your spirit a regular dose of nourishment. It helps you stay connected to your purpose, process your emotions in real time, and keep from getting too weighed down by life's inevitable ups and downs. Think of it as an anchor, keeping you steady when the waves get choppy.

Without a consistent practice, it's easy to drift. Life gets busy, distractions pop up, and before you know it, you're feeling untethered, anxious, and out of sync. A daily spiritual healing routine keeps you grounded, focused, and aligned with what truly matters to you. It becomes a sacred pause, a chance to reconnect with your inner self and re-center before the day begins or ends.

Elements of a Healing Practice

A spiritual practice isn't a one-size-fits-all formula. It should reflect who you are, what you value, and what brings you peace. Here are some foundational elements to consider when creating your own routine:

1. **Setting Intentions**

    Every day is an opportunity for growth, healing, and discovery. Starting your day with a clear intention can help you stay focused on what matters most. Take a few moments each morning to set an intention for the day. It could be as simple as, "Today, I choose peace," or, "I am open to growth and learning."

    Intentions don't have to be grand or complex—they're just little reminders of how you want to show up. Over time, these daily intentions create a powerful thread of purpose that weaves through your life. Setting intentions grounds you and gives you a sense of direction, helping you stay aligned with your values.

2. **Grounding Through Meditation or Breathwork**

    Meditation and breathwork are powerful tools for calming the mind, releasing tension, and connecting with your inner self. Even five minutes can make a difference. If meditation feels daunting, start small. Sit quietly, close your eyes, and focus on your breath. Inhale deeply, hold, then exhale slowly. Let each breath center you, bringing your attention fully into the present.

    If you prefer guided meditation, there are countless resources available—apps, online videos, or simply focusing on a calming word or phrase, like "peace" or "release." Over time, grounding practices like these can help you stay calm, even in stressful situations. Meditation and breathwork are like mini reset buttons, helping you release negative energy and return to a place of inner peace.

3. **Daily Reflection Through Journaling**

Journaling is a sacred space where you can process thoughts, emotions, and insights. It's a way to check in with yourself, to see what's on your mind and in your heart. Each day, take a few minutes to jot down whatever comes up. Don't worry about making it perfect; this is just for you.

Here are a few prompts to get started:

- What am I feeling today?
- What am I grateful for?
- What do I want to let go of?
- How can I grow from today's experiences?

Over time, journaling helps you see patterns, track your growth, and gain insight into what you need to heal and thrive. This daily habit fosters self-awareness and allows you to express yourself freely, without judgment.

4. **Affirmations and Mantras**

Our minds are powerful, and the words we speak to ourselves shape our reality. Affirmations and mantras are positive statements that reinforce your goals, values, and beliefs. Think of them as little pep talks for your spirit. Choose a few affirmations that resonate with you, and repeat them daily.

Some examples might be:

- "I am worthy of love and healing."
- "I trust the journey, even when it's hard."
- "I am resilient, and I can handle whatever comes my way."

You can write them in your journal, say them out loud, or even place sticky notes around your space as reminders. Affirmations may feel strange at first, but over time, they become powerful tools for rewiring your mindset. Each repetition strengthens your belief in yourself and aligns your thoughts with your desired reality.

5. **Mindful Movement**

   Moving your body is a way to release stored tension, process emotions, and connect with yourself physically. This doesn't have to mean an intense workout—think gentle stretching, yoga, a walk outside, or dancing to your favorite song. The goal is to move with awareness, to tune in to how your body feels, and to let movement bring you a sense of peace and release.

   Try starting your day with a few minutes of stretching or end your day with a mindful walk. Movement, when done with intention, can be a powerful way to ground yourself. It brings you back into your body, allowing you to release physical tension and feel present in the moment.

6. **Creating a Sacred Space**

   Having a dedicated space for your spiritual practice can make it feel even more special. This could be a corner of a room, a shelf with items that inspire you, or a full meditation space. Include objects that have personal significance—crystals, candles, photos, anything that brings you comfort.

   Your sacred space doesn't need to be elaborate. It's just a place where you feel safe, peaceful, and connected. Returning to this space each day can help signal to your mind and body that it's time for healing, reflection, and growth. This space becomes a physical reminder of your commitment to self-care and inner peace.

7. **Gratitude Practice**

   Gratitude has an almost magical way of shifting our focus from what's wrong to what's right. Every day, take a few moments to write down or think about three things you're grateful for. They don't have to be big—sometimes the small things are the most meaningful. Maybe it's the warm cup of coffee you enjoyed, the laugh you shared with a friend, or the simple fact that you have a safe place to call home.

   Gratitude doesn't ignore challenges; it simply helps you see the beauty alongside the struggle. A regular gratitude practice can help you feel more positive, grounded, and connected to life. It reminds you that, even in difficult times, there is always something to appreciate.

Designing Your Practice: Tips for Success

Your spiritual healing practice should feel like a gift to yourself, not another item on your to-do list. Here are some tips to make it meaningful and sustainable:

- **Start Small**: Don't try to do everything at once. Begin with one or two elements that resonate most, then gradually add more as it feels right.

- **Be Consistent, Not Perfect**: The goal is progress, not perfection. Some days, you'll miss a practice, or it won't feel as powerful. That's okay. Consistency matters more than getting it "right" every time.

- **Adjust as Needed**: Your practice should evolve with you. As you grow, your needs will change. Don't be afraid to switch things up, add new elements, or let go of parts that no longer serve you.

- **Celebrate Small Wins**: Recognize the effort you're putting in, even on the days it feels small. Each time you show up for yourself, you're reinforcing a powerful habit of self-love and healing.

Making Your Practice a Sacred Part of Your Day

Incorporating spiritual healing into your daily life isn't about following a strict routine; it's about creating a rhythm that feels natural, nurturing, and meaningful. Think of your practice as a daily appointment with your soul—a time when you reconnect with what matters, check in with yourself, and lay the foundation for ongoing growth.

Building a Practice That Lasts

Remember, there's no "one way" to do this. Your spiritual practice should feel personal, flexible, and supportive of where you are on your journey. You're allowed to experiment, to find what works, and to let go of anything that doesn't resonate. This is your sacred space, your path to healing, and your opportunity to reconnect with yourself every single day.

In the next chapter, we'll explore the art of releasing old wounds and breaking harmful patterns, so you can continue moving forward with strength, clarity, and freedom. This is where your practice becomes a catalyst for deep, lasting transformation. Get ready to dive even deeper!

Chapter 8

Healing Past Wounds and Breaking Patterns
Letting Go of the Past and Setting Yourself Free

We all have a past. And for many of us, that past holds moments that feel too heavy, memories that linger too long, and patterns that keep showing up like an uninvited guest. Healing past wounds and breaking unhealthy patterns is one of the most challenging—and most rewarding—steps on the path of soul growth. It's about taking the lessons and leaving the pain behind, about honoring where you've been without letting it dictate where you're going.

In this chapter, we'll look at practical, compassionate ways to heal old wounds and let go of the patterns that no longer serve you. It's time to release the past and start living fully in the present.

Understanding the Impact of Old Wounds

Wounds from our past often leave marks that run deep. These wounds shape our beliefs about ourselves, others, and the world around us. If left unhealed, they can become patterns—repeating cycles of behavior, thoughts, or emotions that keep us stuck.

Imagine you've got an invisible backpack, and every unresolved hurt or painful memory is a rock weighing you down. Over time, these rocks add up, making it hard to move forward. But when you choose to heal, you start taking those rocks out, lightening the load. You're reclaiming your energy, your freedom, and your future. Healing means acknowledging the pain, understanding its impact, and choosing to release it.

Breaking Patterns: Identifying Your Cycles

One of the first steps in healing is recognizing the patterns that hold you back. Patterns might look like:

- Repeatedly choosing similar, unhealthy relationships
- Self-sabotage whenever you get close to success
- Struggling with self-worth or constantly doubting yourself

These cycles don't define who you are; they're just habits of thought or behavior that you picked up along the way. And the best part? Once you become aware of them, you can change them. Awareness is the first step toward breaking free. It's about noticing where you feel "stuck" and daring to ask yourself why.

Exercise: Identify and Name Your Patterns

Grab a journal and jot down any repeating patterns you notice in your life. Think about relationships, self-talk, habits, and ways you respond to stress. Give each pattern a name, like "Perfectionist Pressure" or "Fear of Abandonment." Naming them helps you separate these patterns from your identity—they're something you can change, not something you are. By naming them, you're beginning the process of taking control.

The Power of Forgiveness: Letting Go of What Hurts

Forgiveness is a cornerstone of healing, but let's be clear—it's not about excusing hurtful behavior or pretending everything's okay. Forgiveness is about freeing yourself. It's a gift you give to yourself, allowing you to let go of resentment and reclaim the energy that's tied up in old wounds.

Forgiveness can be challenging, especially if the pain runs deep. Start by asking yourself if there's anything or anyone you need to forgive—including yourself. Then, take it one step at a time. Forgiveness is a journey, not a quick fix. It's an act of courage and self-compassion.

Exercise: The Forgiveness Letter

Write a letter to someone you feel hurt by, even if you never send it. Pour out everything—your pain, anger, and what you wish they had understood. Then, when you're ready, write a statement of forgiveness. It could be as simple as, "I forgive you, and I release the hold this memory has on me." You don't need to send the letter; the act of writing and forgiving is for you, to set you free. This exercise is a way to honor your feelings, express them fully, and choose to release them.

Shadow Work: Embracing and Healing Your "Shadow Self"

The "shadow self" is a concept introduced by psychologist Carl Jung. It refers to the parts of ourselves we've buried—the traits, emotions, and experiences we find difficult to accept. Often, these shadows stem from wounds, fears, or beliefs we adopted in response to pain.

Healing the shadow self is about embracing all of who you are, even the parts you've tried to ignore or push away. It's about shining light on the shadow, acknowledging it, and finding compassion for the parts of yourself that are hurting. When you make peace with your shadow, you reclaim parts of yourself you've been at war with.

Exercise: Meeting Your Shadow Self

Close your eyes, take a few deep breaths, and imagine a younger version of yourself sitting across from you. This is a part of you that's been carrying pain or fear. Ask this part of yourself what it needs, what it's afraid of, and why it feels the way it does. Listen without judgment, and offer compassion. Visualize wrapping this younger self in kindness and love, letting them know they're safe and valued. This visualization helps you connect with and soothe the parts of you that still feel wounded.

Breaking Free: Cutting Energetic Ties

Sometimes, old wounds are tied to specific people, places, or events. These connections can feel like invisible cords that keep you attached to the past. Cutting these energetic ties doesn't mean forgetting or denying what happened—it's a way to release the emotional grip it has on you.

Exercise: Cord-Cutting Visualization

Find a quiet space, close your eyes, and take a few deep breaths. Visualize the person, memory, or experience that you want to release. Imagine a cord connecting you to it. When you're ready, visualize yourself gently cutting the cord, releasing it with love and compassion. Repeat a phrase like, "I release this with love. I am free." This visualization helps you symbolically let go, creating a sense of freedom and closure.

Replacing Old Patterns with Empowering New Ones

As you release old patterns and wounds, it's important to replace them with positive, empowering behaviors. Healing isn't just about letting go; it's also about filling that space with something new. If you used to cope with stress through self-doubt, maybe your new habit becomes self-affirmation. If you tended to settle for less in relationships, your new pattern might be setting boundaries.

Choose one new habit or pattern that represents the person you want to become. Maybe it's speaking kindly to yourself, embracing vulnerability, or pursuing your goals with courage. Each small action is a step toward building a life that's free from the weight of past wounds.

Exercise: Your New Empowering Habit

Choose one area where you'd like to break an old pattern. Then, think about what new habit or belief you can practice to replace it. Write it down, and create a small, daily action to reinforce it. For example, if you're replacing self-doubt, your action might be saying an affirmation each morning: "I am capable, and I trust myself."

Consistency is key; each time you practice your new habit, you're reshaping your mindset.

Celebrating Progress and Growth

Healing isn't a one-time event; it's a lifelong journey. As you work through past wounds and break old patterns, remember to celebrate your progress. Each step forward is a victory, even if it feels small. Healing isn't about reaching a final destination—it's about becoming more connected, compassionate, and free.

Take time to recognize how far you've come. Celebrate the small wins: the day you set a boundary, the moment you let go of an old hurt, the choice to choose self-love over self-criticism. These small acts of healing add up to big transformation over time.

Moving Forward: Living Free from the Past

Breaking free from old wounds and patterns doesn't mean you'll never think about them again. They're part of your story, but they no longer have to define your future. As you let go, you make space for new experiences, healthier relationships, and greater self-love.

In the next chapter, we'll dive into cultivating self-love and empowerment—an essential part of maintaining the freedom you've worked so hard to create. By honoring yourself, trusting in your resilience, and embracing the person you're becoming, you'll continue to grow into a life that feels truly, deeply yours.

Chapter 9

Soul Growth Through Self-Love and Empowerment
Building a Foundation of Compassion, Confidence, and True Strength

Self-love. It's a term that's been thrown around so much it almost sounds cliché, but don't let the buzzwords fool you—self-love and empowerment are the true building blocks of lasting soul growth. Without them, healing can feel like patching a cracked foundation. Self-love is about honoring your worth, embracing who you are, and empowering yourself to create a life that reflects your deepest values and desires.

This chapter is all about cultivating a compassionate relationship with yourself, breaking free from self-criticism, and building confidence that can weather any storm. Get ready to step into the fullest version of you—strong, empowered, and unapologetically authentic.

What Is Self-Love, Really?

Self-love isn't about vanity, arrogance, or ignoring your flaws. It's about creating a relationship with yourself that's based on respect, kindness, and acceptance. Self-love means being willing to see all of who you are—the light and the shadow—and loving yourself anyway. It's about recognizing your inherent worth and letting go of the need for external validation.

In practical terms, self-love shows up in the choices you make, the boundaries you set, and the way you speak to yourself. It's not a one-time decision; it's a daily practice that allows you to grow, heal, and thrive. Self-love is an act of courage, a choice to prioritize your well-being, and a commitment to treat yourself with the same kindness you offer to others.

Breaking the Cycle of Self-Criticism

Many of us are our own harshest critics. We carry around an internal dialogue that's more brutal than any external judgment. Whether it's doubting your abilities, criticizing your appearance, or rehashing mistakes, self-criticism can be a major barrier to growth.

But here's the truth: You're not helping yourself by being hard on yourself. Self-criticism drains your energy, lowers your confidence, and keeps you stuck in a loop of shame and guilt. The good news is that you can shift this inner dialogue.

Exercise: Turning Self-Criticism into Self-Compassion

The next time you catch yourself being self-critical, pause and ask yourself, "Would I say this to a friend?" If the answer is no, reframe it with kindness. For example:

- Instead of "I'm such a failure," try "I'm doing my best, and that's enough."
- Instead of "I can't believe I messed that up," try "I'm learning and growing through this experience."

Each time you practice self-compassion, you're building a more positive, supportive relationship with yourself. Self-compassion isn't about avoiding responsibility; it's about embracing your humanity and acknowledging that growth is a journey.

Setting Boundaries as a Form of Self-Love

Setting boundaries is one of the most empowering acts of self-love. Boundaries are limits that protect your energy, your time, and your emotional well-being. They're not about shutting people out—they're about honoring your needs and values.

Maybe you've struggled with saying no, or you've let people overstep your boundaries because you didn't want to disappoint them. But true self-love means recognizing that you deserve respect, and sometimes that means saying no, setting limits, and protecting your peace.

Exercise: Creating a "Boundaries List"

Make a list of areas in your life where you feel your boundaries need reinforcement. These might be relationships, work commitments, or even personal habits. Next to each item, write down one action you can take to strengthen that boundary. It could be a phrase you'll practice saying, like "I don't have the capacity for this right now," or a small change in your routine that prioritizes your needs. Boundaries remind you that it's okay to prioritize yourself and that doing so is essential for your well-being.

Building Confidence from Within

Confidence doesn't come from others' approval or external success; it comes from a deep trust in yourself. True confidence is knowing that no matter what happens, you have your own back. It's believing in your worth, even when things don't go according to plan.

If confidence feels elusive, start by celebrating small wins. Each time you follow through on a commitment, make a decision based on your intuition, or choose self-care over self-sacrifice, you're reinforcing that inner confidence.

Exercise: Celebrating Small Wins

At the end of each day, write down one thing you did that you're proud of. It doesn't have to be a big accomplishment—maybe it was setting a boundary, showing up for yourself, or simply getting through a tough day. This practice reminds you of your strength and reinforces self-trust. Celebrating small wins builds momentum and reminds you of the resilience you carry within.

Cultivating Self-Love Through Daily Affirmations

Affirmations are powerful tools for rewiring your mindset and reinforcing self-love. By repeating positive, empowering statements, you're creating new neural pathways that support a more compassionate view of yourself. Affirmations might feel a little awkward at first, but over time, they can become a meaningful part of your routine.

Exercise: Creating Your Own Affirmations

Write down three to five affirmations that resonate with you. These should be statements that reinforce your worth, your resilience, and your growth. Examples include:

- "I am worthy of love, respect, and happiness."
- "I am strong, resilient, and capable."
- "I honor my journey and trust in my growth."

Repeat these affirmations each morning or whenever you need a boost. You can write them on sticky notes, keep them in your phone, or say them out loud as part of your daily practice. Affirmations help redirect your mind toward self-empowerment and away from self-doubt.

Practicing Self-Care as an Act of Empowerment

Self-care isn't just about spa days and bubble baths (though those are wonderful too). It's about prioritizing your needs, taking time to recharge, and recognizing that you deserve kindness from yourself. Self-care is an empowering choice that signals to yourself that you matter.

Make self-care a non-negotiable part of your routine. Whether it's taking five minutes to breathe, setting aside time for a hobby, or creating a nourishing morning ritual, self-care is an act of empowerment that fuels your growth.

Exercise: Creating a Self-Care Plan

List three activities that make you feel grounded, nourished, and happy. Schedule time for at least one of these activities each week. Self-care doesn't have to be elaborate; it just needs to be intentional. By making it a priority, you're reinforcing your own worth and well-being.

Embracing Your Authentic Self

True empowerment comes from embracing who you are—unfiltered, imperfect, and real. When you accept yourself fully, you step into a place of authenticity. You're no longer trying to fit someone else's mold or live up to unrealistic standards. Instead, you're honoring your unique journey and trusting that who you are is enough.

Embracing your authentic self means letting go of the need to please others or seek approval. It's about showing up as you are, with all your strengths and quirks, and knowing that you are worthy just as you are.

Exercise: Writing a Love Letter to Yourself

Sit down with a piece of paper and write a love letter to yourself. Acknowledge the qualities you appreciate, the challenges you've overcome, and the dreams you hold. Remind yourself that you are worthy of love and respect. Keep this letter somewhere you can read it whenever you need a reminder of your strength and beauty.

Empowering Yourself to Live Boldly

Self-love isn't just about feeling good—it's about empowering yourself to live boldly. When you love and accept yourself, you open the door to new possibilities, experiences, and connections. You're no longer living from a place of fear or self-doubt; you're living from a place of courage and authenticity.

Living boldly means:

- • Pursuing your passions without fear of judgment
- • Speaking your truth, even when it's uncomfortable
- • Setting goals that reflect your deepest desires
- • Embracing the unknown with an open heart

Empowerment isn't about eliminating fear; it's about moving forward despite it. Each time you choose courage over comfort, you're strengthening your confidence and building a life that feels deeply aligned with your soul.

Moving Forward: Self-Love as a Lifelong Journey

Self-love and empowerment aren't destinations—they're ongoing journeys. Some days, you'll feel strong and confident; other days, self-doubt will creep in. That's okay. The key is to keep showing up for yourself, to keep nurturing the relationship you have with yourself, and to remember that self-love is a practice.

As you move forward, know that each act of kindness you extend to yourself, each boundary you set, and each moment of courage is a step toward a life of true soul growth.

In the next chapter, we'll explore the role of gratitude and joy in healing, and how celebrating the beauty of life can deepen your connection to yourself and the world around you. Get ready to embrace the power of gratitude and the magic of everyday joy.

Chapter 10

Embracing Gratitude and Finding Joy Amid Setbacks
Celebrating Life's Small Moments to Fuel Healing and Growth

Gratitude and joy—two simple, beautiful forces that have the power to transform how we experience life, especially when things get tough. When setbacks and challenges arise, it's easy to focus on what's wrong and let those difficulties overshadow everything else. But when we choose gratitude and seek out moments of joy, we create a shift in perspective that helps us weather life's storms with grace, resilience, and a sense of purpose.

In this chapter, we'll explore the healing power of gratitude and joy, how to make them a daily practice, and why celebrating life's small moments can become the fuel that keeps you going.

Why Gratitude Matters (Especially During Hard Times)

Gratitude is more than just a feel-good exercise; it's a powerful way to reframe your mindset, helping you see beauty and meaning in everyday life. When things get difficult, gratitude acts as a grounding force, reminding you of what's still good and true, even amid the chaos.

Research has shown that gratitude can reduce stress, increase happiness, and even improve physical health. But beyond the science, gratitude is a practice of presence—it draws your attention to the moment and helps you appreciate the blessings you already have. And in a world that often feels focused on what's missing or what's wrong, gratitude is a radical act of positivity.

How to Cultivate a Gratitude Practice

Gratitude doesn't have to be complicated or time-consuming. Here are some simple ways to make gratitude part of your daily life:

1. **Daily Gratitude Journaling**

    Set aside a few minutes each day to write down three things you're grateful for. They can be small—a warm cup of coffee, a good conversation, the comfort of a cozy blanket—or big, like the love of family or the opportunity to pursue a dream. By writing them down, you're training your mind to look for blessings in every day.

2. **Gratitude in the Moment**

    When something good happens, take a few seconds to fully appreciate it. Let yourself feel the joy or relief, even in the smallest moments. By practicing gratitude in the moment, you're creating a habit of appreciation that can help you see beauty in the present.

3. **Gratitude Reminders**

    Set reminders on your phone or place sticky notes around your home to prompt you to pause and feel grateful. These reminders can be simple phrases like, "Take a breath and notice the good," or "What am I grateful for right now?" Over time, these prompts help gratitude become an automatic part of your mindset.

The Healing Power of Finding Joy

Joy might feel like a distant idea when you're going through a tough time, but it's often the very thing we need to reconnect with life and our own resilience. Joy isn't just about being happy; it's about savoring moments that bring lightness, wonder, and connection. When we seek out and celebrate moments of joy, we're giving ourselves permission to experience life fully, even amid struggles.

Practical Ways to Cultivate Joy

Joy doesn't have to come from big, grand events. Often, it's found in the smallest, simplest moments. Here's how to invite more joy into your life:

1. **Engage in Activities You Love**

   Make a list of things that bring you joy, no matter how small or silly they may seem. Dancing, cooking, painting, listening to music, taking a walk in nature—whatever it is, carve out time to do these things regularly. Joy is often found in moments of self-expression and creativity, where you're fully present and free.

2. **Practice Mindful Presence**

   Joy is about being present. When you're truly engaged in the moment, whether it's enjoying a meal or having a good laugh with a friend, joy flows naturally. Try to notice the details—the colors, sounds, smells, and feelings—around you. Being mindful opens the door to joy, even in ordinary moments.

3. **Celebrate Small Wins**

   Every step forward, no matter how small, is worth celebrating. Maybe you finished a project, set a boundary, or tried something new. Recognize these small victories, and let yourself feel proud. Celebrating your progress reinforces a positive mindset and encourages you to keep going.

Bringing Gratitude and Joy Together

Gratitude and joy go hand in hand. Gratitude helps us recognize the blessings in our lives, and joy is the expression of that recognition. By practicing both, you create a cycle of positive energy that fuels your growth, strengthens your resilience, and brings light into even the darkest days.

Exercise: The Gratitude and Joy Journal

Create a dedicated journal or section in your journal where you record moments of gratitude and joy each day. Here's how it might look:

- **Gratitude**: Write down three things you're grateful for today.
- **Joy**: Note one moment of joy you experienced, no matter how small.

This simple practice helps you cultivate both gratitude and joy daily, creating a habit of positivity that grows over time.

Shifting Your Focus from "What's Missing" to "What's Here"

One of the biggest barriers to joy and gratitude is a focus on lack. It's easy to get caught up in what we don't have, what we wish was different, or what we feel is missing. But when you consciously shift your focus to what's already here, you begin to see abundance instead of scarcity.

Each day, try to notice when your mind drifts toward what's lacking, and gently bring it back to what's present. This shift doesn't ignore challenges; it simply helps you see that life's blessings coexist with life's struggles.

Cultivating Joy Amid Setbacks

Joy during setbacks might feel impossible, but it's about finding small moments of lightness and relief that keep you going. Here are some ways to find joy, even in tough times:

- **Laugh (Even if You Don't Feel Like It)**: Watch a funny show, call a friend with a great sense of humor, or read something that makes you smile. Laughter is one of the simplest ways to reconnect with joy.
- **Seek Comfort in Routine**: Sometimes, joy is found in the familiar. Engaging in daily routines like making tea, reading a book, or taking a short walk can bring moments of peace and stability.
- **Allow Yourself Little Treats**: Whether it's a favorite snack, a hot bath, or a cozy blanket, small comforts can bring joy. Don't underestimate the power of little indulgences to lift your spirit.

Embracing Gratitude as a Lifelong Practice

Gratitude isn't just a tool for getting through hard times—it's a way of seeing the world. By making gratitude a lifelong practice, you're creating a mindset that can find beauty, even in unexpected places. Gratitude reminds you that life, with all its highs and lows, is something to be celebrated.

Each time you choose gratitude, you're choosing to see the fullness of life rather than just its challenges. You're creating a foundation of positivity that will support you through every season, every setback, and every moment of growth.

Celebrating the Gift of Now

In the end, gratitude and joy are about being present—about embracing the gift of this moment, no matter what it holds. When you live with gratitude and seek out joy, you're choosing to see life not as a series of obstacles, but as a journey filled with meaning, beauty, and connection.

Remember that you don't need to wait for everything to be perfect to feel grateful or joyful. The perfect time to embrace gratitude and joy is now, exactly where you are.

Moving Forward: Letting Joy and Gratitude Lead the Way

As you continue your journey of healing and growth, let gratitude and joy be your guides. Trust that these practices will help you navigate the hard times and enrich the good ones. By choosing gratitude and joy daily, you're building a life filled with love, resilience, and soul-deep satisfaction.

In the final chapter, we'll explore how to integrate everything you've learned and keep moving forward on your journey of soul growth, with purpose, confidence, and an open heart. Get ready to step fully into the next chapter of your life, empowered and transformed.

Chapter 11

Moving Forward: Integrating Growth and Embracing the Journey
Living with Purpose, Confidence, and an Open Heart

As you reach this stage of your journey, take a moment to acknowledge everything you've learned and how far you've come. You've dived deep into healing old wounds, embraced self-love, cultivated resilience, and built a daily practice of gratitude and joy. Each step has added to your foundation, giving you a toolkit for handling life's challenges with grace, strength, and a sense of purpose. Yet, growth doesn't stop here. This chapter is about integrating all the lessons and practices you've developed, turning them into a way of life. Moving forward, you'll continue to evolve, encounter new experiences, and refine your path. Life is an ongoing journey, and you're ready to walk it with confidence, courage, and an open heart.

Embracing Your Journey as a Process, Not a Destination

It's natural to think of healing and growth as something with a finish line, a place where you'll finally "arrive." But the truth is, soul growth is a lifelong journey. There will always be new layers to uncover, new lessons to learn, and new experiences that shape you. Embracing this mindset allows you to approach life with curiosity and flexibility, rather than pressure or perfectionism. Moving forward, remind yourself that growth is not a linear path. There will be setbacks, breakthroughs, pauses, and leaps. Each stage has value and wisdom to offer. Trust that you're exactly where you're meant to be and that each part of your journey has a purpose.

Cultivating Self-Awareness and Adaptability

As you integrate growth, consider cultivating self-awareness as a daily practice. Self-awareness helps you understand your motivations, your reactions, and your values more deeply. Adaptability, on the other hand, helps you respond to life's twists and turns with resilience. Together, these qualities empower you to meet any situation from a place of understanding and flexibility, allowing you to embrace change rather than resist it.

Integrating Daily Practices into Your Life

By now, you've developed practices that help you stay grounded, centered, and connected to your purpose. Whether it's journaling, setting intentions, expressing gratitude, or engaging in mindful movement, these habits are tools to keep you aligned with your highest self. Here are some tips for making these practices a permanent part of your life:

1. **Start Your Day with Intention**

    Begin each day with a moment of stillness to set an intention. Ask yourself, "How do I want to show up today?" Setting an intention each morning helps you focus on what truly matters and keeps you aligned with your values and goals.

2. **Reflect and Realign Weekly**

    Take time once a week to reflect on your journey. Consider what went well, what challenged you, and where you want to grow. Weekly reflections help you stay aware of patterns, reinforce positive habits, and course-correct as needed.

3. **Create a "Soul Growth" Check-In**

    Every few months, set aside time for a deeper check-in. Review your progress, celebrate how far you've come, and consider what's next on your journey. This practice keeps you connected to your path and allows you to adjust your goals as you evolve.

Living in Alignment with Your Purpose

One of the most powerful gifts of healing is the clarity it brings. As you've moved through this journey, you've connected with your purpose and begun to understand what truly matters to you. Moving forward, let your purpose guide your choices, relationships, and commitments. Living in alignment with your purpose doesn't mean every decision will be easy, but it gives you a compass—a sense of direction that helps you navigate life with confidence. When you're faced with decisions, ask yourself, "Does this align with who I am and who I want to become?" This simple question can help you stay true to yourself and avoid choices that pull you away from your purpose.

Staying Open to New Lessons and Growth

Healing isn't a one-time event; it's a continuous process. Life will keep presenting opportunities for growth, and each experience—whether joyful or challenging—has something to teach. Stay open to these lessons. Even when a situation feels like a setback, remember that it could be an opportunity to deepen your resilience, strengthen your compassion, or clarify your values.

Exercise: Reflection on Life's Lessons

Take a moment to reflect on a recent experience, positive or difficult. Ask yourself:

- What did this experience teach me about myself?
- How can I use this lesson to grow?
- What is one small way I can integrate this insight into my life? This exercise helps you see life as a teacher, guiding you toward growth, even in the most unexpected ways.

Finding Meaning in Every Season of Life

Life is made up of seasons—times of growth, times of rest, times of challenge, and times of celebration. Each season has value and contributes to your journey.

Trust that even in periods of waiting or uncertainty, you're still moving forward. Some of the most profound growth happens in quiet, reflective seasons when you're processing, healing, and preparing for what's next. Instead of rushing through difficult times or wishing for "the next thing," try to find meaning in the present. Each season, with its unique challenges and blessings, is shaping you into the person you're meant to be.

Practicing Acceptance and Letting Go

As you continue your journey, remember that acceptance and letting go are essential parts of soul growth. Not everything will go as planned, and not every outcome will align with your expectations. Sometimes, letting go is the most powerful act of love you can offer yourself—releasing control, trusting the process, and making peace with what is. Letting go doesn't mean giving up; it means releasing the need for certainty and embracing life's flow. It's about trusting that each experience has a purpose, even if it's not immediately clear. With practice, acceptance and letting go become tools for peace and freedom, allowing you to move forward without the weight of unmet expectations.

Building a Supportive Community

Growth is a journey best taken in good company. Surround yourself with people who support, inspire, and challenge you. These are the friends, mentors, and loved ones who celebrate your victories, help you see your potential, and encourage you during tough times. Seek out like-minded souls who share your values and are committed to their own growth. A supportive community gives you strength, perspective, and a safe space to share your journey. Remember, you're not alone on this path—there are others walking alongside you, each on their own unique journey of growth.

Celebrating the Person You've Become

One of the most important parts of moving forward is recognizing and celebrating the person you've become. You've done the hard work of healing, let go of past hurts, and stepped into a place of greater self-love, resilience, and purpose. Take time to honor your journey and acknowledge the progress you've made. Celebrate the small victories, the inner strength you've cultivated, and the courage it took to face your shadows. You're not the same person you were when you started this journey, and that deserves recognition. Let this celebration be a reminder of your capacity for growth and your commitment to living fully.

Looking Ahead with Hope and Confidence

As you continue your journey, keep looking forward with hope and confidence. Trust that life will keep offering new opportunities for growth, healing, and discovery. Embrace the unknown, knowing that you're equipped with the tools, resilience, and wisdom to face whatever comes your way. Life will always present challenges, but you've shown yourself that you have the strength to overcome them. Moving forward, let your heart stay open, your spirit stay curious, and your soul stay grounded. This is your journey, and you're exactly where you need to be.

Final Reflection: Embracing the Journey with Grace

Take a deep breath. Feel the weight of everything you've released, the strength you've built, and the lightness of stepping into a future that reflects your true self. This journey has been one of transformation, growth, and healing, and it will continue to unfold in beautiful, unexpected ways. As you step forward, let grace guide you. Embrace the journey, trust in yourself, and remember that you are capable of incredible growth, healing, and love. This is the beginning of a lifelong adventure, one that will lead you to new depths of understanding, purpose, and joy. Thank you for embracing this journey with courage, compassion, and an open heart. Keep moving forward, trusting that the best is yet to come.

Chapter 12

Embracing Your Power and Living Fully
Stepping into Your Authentic Self and Creating a Life You Love

As you reach the end of this journey—and the beginning of so many others—take a moment to reflect on everything you've discovered. You've faced challenges, learned to let go, cultivated resilience, embraced self-love, and uncovered a sense of purpose. You've learned the art of seeing setbacks as stepping stones, of finding gratitude and joy in every season, and of building a life aligned with your soul's deepest values. This final chapter is about stepping fully into your power, living authentically, and creating a life that feels rich with meaning. It's a reminder that you hold the power to shape your path and to continue growing, evolving, and healing for the rest of your life.

Embracing Your Authentic Self

Living fully starts with embracing who you are, unfiltered and unapologetic. It means releasing the need to conform, to please others, or to fit into someone else's expectations. Instead, you're choosing to honor your own voice, trust your intuition, and live in alignment with your values. Authenticity is about letting yourself be seen, flaws and all, and recognizing that you're worthy of love, respect, and happiness exactly as you are. It's about moving forward with confidence in your own uniqueness and knowing that your true self is your greatest asset.

Exercise: Your Authenticity Statement

Take a moment to write a statement that captures who you are and what you stand for. This could be a few words, a phrase, or a sentence. Let it reflect your values, your vision, and the kind of life you want to lead. Keep this statement somewhere you'll see it often, as a reminder to stay true to yourself.

Creating a Vision for Your Future

Now that you've cleared old patterns, built new habits, and connected with your purpose, it's time to dream big. What do you want to create, experience, and become? Take time to imagine the life you truly desire—a life that reflects your values, honors your growth, and brings you joy. Creating a vision for your future isn't about rigid goals or expectations. It's about setting intentions that inspire and guide you. Your vision is your roadmap, helping you stay aligned with what truly matters to you, even as life changes and evolves.

Exercise: Vision Board or Future Journal

Create a vision board or write a "future journal" entry describing your ideal life. Include everything that feels meaningful to you—relationships, career, personal growth, health, adventure, creativity. Let your imagination flow without limitation. This vision is a reflection of your soul's deepest desires, a guiding light for the path ahead.

Practicing Courage in Everyday Life

Living fully requires courage—the courage to take risks, to pursue your passions, to face your fears, and to embrace change. You don't need to make dramatic shifts or take huge leaps every day. Courage is often found in the small, quiet moments when you choose to follow your heart, stand up for yourself, or step into the unknown. Remember that courage isn't the absence of fear; it's moving forward despite it. Every time you choose courage, you're reinforcing your strength and expanding your comfort zone. With each courageous step, you're creating a life that feels true to who you are.

Exercise: Daily Courage Practice

Each morning, set a small intention to practice courage that day. It could be speaking up, trying something new, or simply honoring a commitment to yourself. At the end of the day, reflect on your courageous act and celebrate your bravery, no matter how small it might feel.

Letting Your Journey Inspire Others

Your journey of growth, healing, and transformation is uniquely yours, but it also has the power to inspire others. By sharing your story, your insights, and your resilience, you can create a ripple effect that empowers those around you. Living authentically and openly can encourage others to do the same, fostering a sense of connection, compassion, and shared growth. You don't need to be a public speaker or writer to inspire others. Simply showing up as your authentic self, being kind, and offering support can be incredibly powerful. Your journey is a gift, and sharing it, even in small ways, can light the way for others.

Celebrating Life Every Step of the Way

Life is meant to be celebrated—not just the big milestones, but the small, everyday moments that make up the journey. Celebrate your growth, your resilience, your victories, and even your struggles. Every part of your journey has value and is worthy of recognition. By choosing to live with a spirit of celebration, you're choosing to honor the beauty of the present moment. Joy isn't something we have to chase; it's something we create by being fully present and appreciative of where we are.

Staying Committed to Growth, Healing, and Joy

The journey of soul growth doesn't end; it's a lifelong path. As you move forward, stay committed to nurturing your spirit, following your intuition, and seeking joy in every season. Trust that each step, no matter how small, is bringing you closer to the life you're meant to live. You'll continue to grow, evolve, and encounter new challenges. And with each experience, you'll deepen your understanding, strengthen your resilience, and expand your capacity for love and compassion. This commitment to growth isn't just a gift to yourself—it's a gift to everyone around you, as you show what it means to live fully, with courage, and an open heart.

Final Reflection: A Love Letter to Your Journey

Take a moment to look back at everything you've experienced, learned, and embraced on this journey. Write a love letter to yourself, expressing gratitude for the courage it took to heal, grow, and transform. Honor the parts of yourself that showed up even when it was hard, that kept going when it felt like too much, and that believed in the possibility of a brighter future. Your journey is a testament to your strength, resilience, and beauty. Carry this love with you as you step into the next chapter of your life. Let it remind you that you are enough, just as you are, and that you have the power to create a life that feels deeply, authentically yours.

Moving Forward: Living a Life of Purpose and Freedom

As you close this chapter and begin the next, remember that you are equipped with everything you need to create a life of purpose, joy, and freedom. You have the tools, the resilience, and the clarity to face whatever comes your way. Trust yourself, honor your journey, and stay open to the magic of growth and transformation. You are ready to live fully, to love deeply, and to walk forward with confidence. Embrace the beauty of your unique path, and let the journey unfold in all its unexpected, wonderful ways. Thank you for embracing this journey with courage, compassion, and an open heart. The world is a brighter, richer place with you in it.

Now, go out and live the life that was always meant to be yours. This is only the beginning of a life filled with purpose, love, and limitless potential. Trust the journey, and remember that you have all the strength, wisdom, and courage you need within you.

Conclusion

A Journey Well Traveled, A Life Ready to Be Lived

As you reach the final page of this book, take a deep, grounding breath. You've walked a powerful journey—one that has led you through self-discovery, healing, and growth. You've faced your shadows, embraced your strengths, and learned to find beauty even in life's most challenging moments. You've transformed setbacks into stepping stones, and you've built a foundation of resilience, joy, and self-love.

But remember, this isn't the end. This journey you're on is lifelong, with new chapters waiting to be written, new insights ready to be discovered, and new layers of growth on the horizon. You now have the tools, the awareness, and the inner strength to meet whatever lies ahead with courage and grace. This book may close here, but your life continues, rich with purpose, authenticity, and the deep understanding that you are capable of living fully, no matter what life brings.

Carry this journey with you, let it inspire you to keep seeking, keep growing, and keep loving yourself every step of the way. You are exactly where you need to be, and you are more than ready to live a life that reflects your truest self. Thank you for walking this path with open-hearted courage and determination. May you continue to rise, heal, and transform, shining your light in a way that only you can.

Appendix

Resources for Continued Growth and Healing

To support you as you continue this journey, here are some resources, tools, and practices you can turn to anytime you need inspiration, guidance, or encouragement. Use this appendix as a quick reference to keep your soul-growth toolkit well-stocked and ready.

1. **Daily Practices and Rituals**

    - Gratitude Journal Prompts:
    - "What are three things I'm grateful for today?"
    - What moment today brought me a sense of peace?"
    - Who in my life am I thankful for, and why?"
    - Morning Intention Setting:
    - Take a moment each morning to set a clear intention. Examples:
    - Today, I choose peace."
    - I am open to growth and learning."
    - I will show kindness to myself and others."
    - Affirmations for Self-Love and Resilience:
    - I am worthy of love and happiness."
      I am growing stronger and wiser each day."
    - I am exactly where I need to be."

2. **Self-Reflection Prompts**
   - Healing Past Wounds:
   - What old patterns am I ready to release?"
   - How can I show compassion to a part of myself that's still healing?"
   - Exploring Your Purpose:
   - What activities make me feel alive and connected to my purpose?"
   - How can I share my gifts to uplift others?"
   - Celebrating Progress:
   - What small victories have I achieved recently?"
   - What strengths have I discovered within myself through this journey?"

3. **Mindfulness and Meditation Tools**
   - Mindfulness Apps: Insight Timer, Calm, Headspace – These apps offer guided meditations, breathing exercises, and relaxation techniques that can help you stay grounded.
   - Breathwork Techniques:
   - 4-7-8 Breathing: Inhale for 4 counts, hold for 7, exhale for 8.
   - Box Breathing: Inhale, hold, exhale, and pause each for 4 counts.

4. **Recommended Reading for Further Growth**

   Self-Love and Empowerment:
   - The Gifts of Imperfection by Brené Brown
   - Radical Acceptance by Tara Brach
   - You Are a Badass by Jen Sincero

Resilience and Healing:

- Rising Strong by Brené Brown
- When Things Fall Apart by Pema Chödrön
- The Body Keeps the Score by Bessel van der Kolk
- Mindfulness and Purpose:
- The Power of Now by Eckhart Tolle
- The Four Agreements by Don Miguel Ruiz
- Man's Search for Meaning by Viktor Frankl

5. **Building a Supportive Community**

   - Online Communities for Personal Growth: Find online support groups, forums, and social media communities that focus on personal development, spiritual growth, and self-care. These can offer encouragement, insights, and a safe space to share your journey.
   - Local Groups and Workshops: Consider joining local meditation groups, book clubs, or self-improvement workshops. Many communities offer gatherings focused on mindfulness, healing, and personal growth.

6. **Journaling Prompts for Continued Reflection**

   Daily Check-In:

   - What am I feeling today, and why?"
   - What would make today feel fulfilling?"
   - End-of-Week Reflection:
   - What challenged me this week, and what did I learn from it?"

- What brought me joy this week, and how can I create more of that?"
- Monthly Reflection:
- What patterns am I noticing in my life right now?"
- How have I grown this month, and what am I grateful for?"

7. Final Words of Encouragement

Remember, healing and growth aren't about perfection. They're about showing up, learning, and growing at your own pace. Keep trusting yourself, keep leaning into the journey, and know that every small step forward counts. You are worthy of all the joy, peace, and fulfillment you seek. As you continue on this path, let these resources serve as reminders of your resilience, your purpose, and the incredible journey you're on.

Thank you for allowing this book to be part of your journey. May you continue to grow, heal, and shine, knowing that you are loved, valued, and deeply capable of creating a life that feels true to your soul. If you have not already please check out my Guided Journal, Journey of My Soul. It has been an honor to write this mini book and I hope you found it helpful.

Much love! -Jamie O'Neill

www.ingramcontent.com/pod-product-compliance
Lightning Source LLC
LaVergne TN
LVHW061048070526
838201LV00074B/5224